Introducing
Jesus

by Tim Chester

Introducing Jesus: life-changing encounters from the Gospel of John
The Good Book Guide to John
© Tim Chester/The Good Book Company, 2010. Reprinted 2012, 2016.
Series Consultants: Tim Chester, Tim Thornborough,
Anne Woodcock, Carl Laferton

The Good Book Company
Tel (UK): 0333 123 0880
Tel (int): + (44) 208 942 0880
Tel: (US): 866 244 2165
Email: info@thegoodbook.co.uk

Websites
UK: www.thegoodbook.co.uk
N America: www.thegoodbook.com
Australia: www.thegoodbook.com.au
New Zealand: www.thegoodbook.co.nz

ISBN: 9781907377129

Printed in the Czech Republic

CONTENTS

Introduction: Good Book Guides

Every Bible-study group is different—yours may take place in a church building, in a home or in a cafe, on a train, over a leisurely mid-morning coffee or squashed into a 30-minute lunch break. Your group may include new Christians, mature Christians, non-Christians, mums and tots, students, businessmen or teens. That's why we've designed these *Good Book Guides* to be flexible for use in many different situations.

Our aim in each session is to uncover the meaning of a passage, and see how it fits into the "big picture" of the Bible. But that can never be the end. We also need to appropriately apply what we have discovered to our lives. Let's take a look at what is included:

Talkabout: Most groups need to "break the ice" at the beginning of a session, and here's the question that will do that. It's designed to get people talking around a subject that will be covered in the course of the Bible study.

Investigate: The Bible text for each session is broken up into manageable chunks, with questions that aim to help you understand what the passage is about. **The Leader's Guide** contains **guidance on questions**, and sometimes ☑ additional "follow-up" questions.

Explore more (optional): These questions will help you connect what you have learned to other parts of the Bible, so you can begin to fit it all together like a jig-saw; or occasionally look at a part of the passage that's not dealt with in detail in the main study.

Apply: As you go through a Bible study, you'll keep coming across **apply** sections. These are questions to get the group discussing what the Bible teaching means in practice for you and your church. ⬓ **Getting personal** is an opportunity for you to think, plan and pray about the changes that you personally may need to make as a result of what you have learned.

Pray: We want to encourage prayer that is rooted in God's word—in line with His concerns, purposes and promises. So each session ends with an opportunity to review the truths and challenges highlighted by the Bible study, and turn them into prayers of request and thanksgiving.

The **Leader's Guide** and introduction provide historical background information, explanations of the Bible texts for each session, ideas for **optional extra** activities, and guidance on how best to help people uncover the truths of God's word.

Why study Introducing Jesus?

It's only when you sit down and talk with someone that you start to discover what they are really like.

What would it be like to have an intimate conversation with Jesus? What would you ask Him? What might He say to you?

In his Gospel, John records for us a series of conversations that Jesus had with different people. They include a confused minister and a desperate woman; a lifelong loser and an anxious politician.

From each conversation there emerges something new about Jesus—who He is, what He came to do and what His priorities and concerns are. And each time we also hear Jesus speaking directly to us. He addresses our doubts and our desires, our fears and our failings, our sorrows and setbacks, and challenges us to think differently about God, life and eternity.

John's Gospel is unique in that it records long and detailed conversations that Jesus had, not just with the crowds and the religious authorities, but also with individuals. We begin to see more clearly the compassion of the Lord Jesus for the many different kinds of people He gave His time to.

But we also see more clearly that He had an agenda for them. He wanted them to see beyond their own horizons—which were limited and lacked perspective—to the greater things that God has in store for those who follow Him.

And Jesus wants to lead us down the same path. To see that there is more to life than what is immediately obvious, that death is not the end, and that the key to fulfilment now, and eternal life for ever, is found in Him alone.

Use these studies to deepen your understanding of Jesus Christ, or perhaps even to be introduced to Him for the first time.

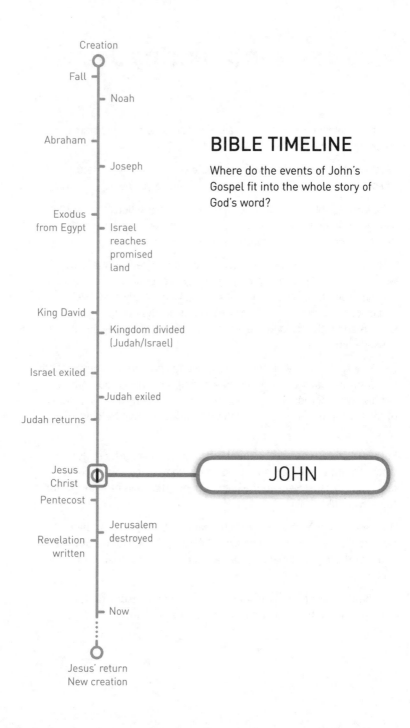

Creation

Fall

Noah

Abraham

Joseph

Exodus from Egypt

Israel reaches promised land

King David

Kingdom divided (Judah/Israel)

Israel exiled

Judah exiled

Judah returns

Jesus Christ

Pentecost

Jerusalem destroyed

Revelation written

Now

Jesus' return
New creation

BIBLE TIMELINE

Where do the events of John's Gospel fit into the whole story of God's word?

JOHN

1

John 3
A CONFUSED MINISTER

⊕ **talkabout**

1. What reasons do people give for ignoring or rejecting Jesus?

⊕ **investigate**

▶ **Read John 3 v 1-10**

Nicodemus was a leading member of the religious establishment and a member of the super-religious group, the Pharisees. Today he might be a vicar—"Nick the Vic". Jesus calls him "Israel's teacher". But what he sees in Jesus confuses him.

2. What is the question behind the statement by Nicodemus in verse 2?

3. How is verse 3 a "reply" to verse 2?

4. What do you need in order to see and enter God's kingdom?

⊡ explore more

In verse 10 Jesus says Nicodemus ought to know about Spirit-transformation because he is a Bible teacher. In other words, he should know that this was promised in the Old Testament.

⊡ Read Ezekiel 36 v 25-27

How does the promise in Ezekiel match the words of Jesus to Nicodemus?
How will the promise in Ezekiel be fulfilled?

⊟ apply

5. What does "born again" mean in our society?

6. What does Jesus mean by being "born again"?

⊡ investigate

⊡ Read John 3 v 10-18

Jesus can speak of "heavenly things" (v 12) like Spirit-transformation because He "came from heaven" (v 11, 13). But Nicodemus can't even understand everyday pictures ("earthly things" in v 12). When it comes to recognising God's kingdom (v 2-3) that's a big problem. It's a big problem because God's King doesn't look anything like what we might expect.

7. Nicodemus is part of the political and religious establishment. What do you think he might expect God's King to be like?

8. We expect a king to be exalted—"lifted up". And God's King will be "lifted up". But what does Jesus actually mean? (See John 12 v 32-33.)

9. Turn to **Numbers 21 v 6-9** to discover the background to verse 14. Why will God's King be exalted or "lifted up" on a cross?

10. What must we do to be saved by God's King?

The reason we don't recognise the crucified King is not just that this is not what we expect an exalted king to look like. It is also what the cross reveals about us: that we are evil people who need a Saviour.

> **Read John 3 v 19-21**

11. See 1 v 1-9. When did God's light come into the world?

12. What stops people "seeing" and coming into God's kingdom?

13. When does this conversation take place and why?

14. How does Jesus interpret the setting that Nicodemus chose for his chat with Jesus?

Nicodemus comes by night and asks: "Why can't I see?"! He is a picture of his own question. Underlying all the reasons we give for not knowing God is the fact that we won't admit our need or submit our lives. And so we need God's Spirit to enable us to recognise God's King because we hide our need for a crucified King.

⇥ apply

15. What does this conversation suggest Christians must do if they want to know God better?

16. What are the implications for our evangelism?

⊡ getting personal

Is there an issue in your life that you are hiding from God? Is there an issue about which you are reluctant to pray? It will stop you enjoying God. "Search me, God, and know my heart; test me and know my anxious thoughts. See if there is any offensive way in me, and lead me in the way everlasting" (Psalm 139 v 23-24).

⬆ pray

Read Psalm 32. Take a verse or two at a time and turn it into prayer.

2 John 4
A DESPERATE WOMAN

⊕ talkabout

1. Think of things that people look to for satisfaction and identity.

⊥ investigate

> **Read John 4 v 1-14**

2. Why is this woman surprised when Jesus asks her for a drink?

3. Why is this woman surprised when Jesus offers her a drink?

4. How does Jesus explain His offer of a drink in verses 13-14?

5. Look at 7 v 37-39. What is the reality that Jesus pictures as "living water"?

❯ Read John 4 v 15-18

It looks like a big change of subject when Jesus asks the woman to fetch her husband. In fact Jesus is going right to the heart of the issue for this woman.

6. How has this woman been trying to satisfy her spiritual thirst?

7. How do we know that this has not brought true and lasting joy?

Jesus offers to satisfy our longings, our desires, our hopes. He promises true identity and fulfilment. The satisfaction that He brings is full instead of partial, and lasting instead of temporary. The maths tells the story for this woman: five husbands plus another man. None of the men in her life have been able to satisfy her desires because those desires are a distorted form of the relationship with God for which we were made.

⤳ apply

8. Look back at your answers to Question One. Many of these things do provide a measure of satisfaction and identity. But evaluate where they lie on a line between partial and full satisfaction, and a line between temporary and lasting satisfaction.

What are the patterns in your life? Where do you keep going to find satisfaction and identity? Are the words "if only" a refrain in your life? What comes after the words "if only"?

God-alternatives provide satisfaction, but only partial and temporary satisfaction. This is why our desires so often draw us deeper into slavery: we need a bigger and bigger fix because we're always left empty. Can you see this pattern in your own life?

⊡ investigate

❯ Read John 4 v 19-24

This time it is the woman who looks as if she's heading off on a tangent. But again Jesus brings the conversation back to the heart of the issue.

DICTIONARY

This mountain (v 20): Mt Gerizim, the centre of Samaritan worship—their equivalent of the temple in Jerusalem for Jews.

9. What does the woman think true worship comes down to?

10. How does Jesus define true worship?

True worship is about where you look for living water to satisfy the thirst of your heart.

❯ Read John 4 v 25-30 and 39-42

11. Look back at verses 6-7. Women collected water in the early morning while it was still cool. Why do you think this woman collects water at the hottest time of the day?

12. Look at verse 29. What does she do after meeting the Messiah?

13. Look at verse 39. What is it that causes the Samaritans to believe in Jesus?

⤷ apply

14. What lessons are there for our evangelism?

⊡ explore more

optional

> **Read John 4 v 31-38**

What are the parallels between this conversation and the conversation between Jesus and the woman? What food does Jesus have to satisfy His spiritual appetite? What invitation does He give to His disciples?

⬆ pray

Read Isaiah 55 v 1-3. Praise God for His gracious invitation. Answer that invitation with your prayers.

3 John 6
A NEEDY CROWD

⊕ talkabout

1. Have you ever known someone get angry with God because God didn't give them what they wanted?

In John 4 we saw that Jesus promises truly to satisfy us. So why does it often seem as if He isn't delivering satisfaction?

⊻ investigate

❯ Read John 6 v 1-15 and v 35

2. John often presents a miracle of Jesus together with some teaching of Jesus so that the teaching explains the miracle. How does verse 35 explain the miraculous feeding of 5,000 men?

> **DICTIONARY**
>
> **Passover Festival (v 4):** a festival commemorating the day God rescued His people from being slaves in Egypt.

❯ Read John 6 v 22-29

3. Why do the crowd come looking for Jesus?

4. What does Jesus offer instead?

> **Read John 6 v 30-34**

5. What does the crowd ask for?

6. How does Jesus respond?

> **Read John 6 v 35-40**

7. What is it is that truly satisfies us eternally?

8. How do we receive true satisfaction?

➡ apply

9. What's wrong with looking to Jesus to satisfy you in the way that the crowd did?

10. What's wrong with wanting bread?

11. The crowd ask for bread in verse 31 with a quote from the Bible. Can you think of examples of people today dressing up selfish desires with pious language?

God gives us many good things. But when those things matter more to us than God, God will not become complicit in our idolatry. God will not fulfil our idolatrous desires because He wants us to desire *Him* above all things. And this is what's best for us because only God Himself brings eternal joy.

⬇ investigate

❯ Read John 6 v 41-51

The crowd can't see past the humanness of Jesus to recognise that He is from heaven. Like Nicodemus in John 3 v 3-8, they need God Himself to enlighten them so that they come to Jesus (see verses 37, 44-45).

12. What happens to those who believe Jesus is the bread of life?

> **Read John 6 v 51-58**

13. Why does Jesus say the living bread is His flesh?

⤷ apply

14. If you live for something other than God, what happens when you don't measure up?

15. If you live for God, what happens when you don't measure up?

⬆ pray

Read verses 66-69 and turn the words of Peter into praise and prayer.

4

A LIFELONG LOSER

⊕ talkabout

1. Who does our society regard as "losers"?

⬇ investigate

In John 9 Jesus has a conversation with a man who was considered by his contemporaries to be a lifelong loser.

▶ Read John 9 v 1-12

2. Why did the disciples think the blind man was a "loser"?

3. Why did Jesus say the man was blind?

4. Look at verses 4-5. What is the day and night to which Jesus refers?

5. How do the events of verses 6-12 explain and prove the claim of Jesus in verse 5?

⤷ apply

6. Look at 9 v 3 and 11 v 4. What do these stories show is one purpose of suffering in our lives?

7. How should this purpose change the way we suffer?

⊡ getting personal

Sometimes people are possessive about their suffering. They use it to make themselves a special case or exempt themselves from responsibilities. How could you use your suffering to bring glory to God?

⊡ explore more

> **Read 1 Corinthians 1 v 26-31**

Who does God choose? Why does God choose them?

optional

⊍ investigate

> **Read John 9 v 13-34**

8. What is the Pharisees' attitude to this healing and to Jesus? How does it change during their conversation with the man born blind?

9. Highlight moments of humour in this conversation.

> **Read John 9 v 35-41**

10. How does the understanding of the man born blind develop during the story?

11. Look at verse 39. How do these words of Jesus provide a commentary on the story?

12. What is the meaning of verse 41?

⤷ apply

13. What are the implications of this story for the way we read the Bible?

14. What does verse 39 suggest happens when we tell people about Jesus?

15. Who are the real "losers" in this story? How might this change the way we view other people?

⤒ pray

Read **2 Corinthians 4 v 4-6**.

- Use verse 5 to pray that you will play your role in mission.
- Use verse 6 to pray that God will play His role in mission.

5 John 11
A GRIEVING FAMILY

⊕ **talkabout**

1. What would you say to someone who has recently been bereaved?

⊥ **investigate**

▶ **Read John 11 v 1-6**

2. What are the similarities in these verses with the story of the man born blind in John 9 (who we looked at in the last session)?

▶ **Read John 11 v 17-27**

3. Look at verses 21-24. What do Martha's words reveal about her faith?

4. Look at verses 25-26. What does Jesus add to her faith in resurrection?

5. What does Jesus mean when He calls Himself "the resurrection and the life", do you think?

6. What response does Jesus look for?

optional

⊡ explore more

> **Read John 3 v 16, 36; 5 v 24-29; 6 v 47-51; 12 v 23-25**

How do these passages reinforce what Jesus says to Martha? What do they add to what Jesus says to Martha?

⊖ apply

7. Martha expresses her confidence in Jesus *before* He has raised Lazarus from the dead. Look at v 45-48. The Jewish leaders reject Jesus *after* they hear of the raising of Lazarus. What does this teach us about true faith?

⊕ investigate

> **Read John 11 v 28-37**

8. How does Jesus respond to Mary?

9. What does Jesus reveal about God's response to bereavement and death?

10. Compare verses 21 and 32. Martha and Mary both greet Jesus with exactly the same words. But Jesus responds very differently. Why do you think this is?

⊡ **apply**

11. What lessons are there for us when we meet bereaved people?

12. Can you think of empty words that we say when people die that do not offer any real comfort?

The words of Jesus are not just empty comfort. They have real substance.

⊡ **investigate**

> **Read John 11 v 38-44**

13. Why does Jesus pray out loud?

14. John 12 v 17-18 describes the raising of Lazarus as a "sign". What does it point to?

⊡ **explore more**

optional

❱ **Read John 12 v 1-3**

How do Martha and Mary respond to the gift of life that Jesus gives? What does this show about how we should respond to Jesus today?

⊡ **getting personal**

Does your faith involve believing there is life after death? Does your faith also involve trusting in the person of Jesus? Does your faith involve feeling close to God when things are going well? Does your faith also involve depending on Jesus in the face of death?

⊡ **pray**

Pray for people you know who are facing death, bereavement or grief at the moment. Pray that they might find comfort in Jesus, the resurrection and the life. And pray that you might be a channel for God's comfort.

6 AN ANXIOUS POLITICIAN

⊕ talkabout

1. What do we expect from spokespeople?

⊕ investigate

> ❯ **Read John 18 v 28-40**

To understand this conversation we need to realise that Pilate and Jesus have completely different understandings of what it means to be a king.

2. What is Pilate's understanding of a king?

3. Look at verse 34. Why does Jesus respond in this way?

4. In verse 36 Jesus answers Pilate's original question about whether He is a king, but how does He redefine what it means to be a king?

5. Look at verse 37. Jesus has come to testify to the truth about God's reign. What was Satan's lie about God's reign in the Garden of Eden (**read Genesis 3 v 1-7**)?

"What is truth?" asks Pilate (verse 38). Perhaps he is mocking Jesus; perhaps he is wistful. Either way he has been playing politics so long he can't remember what truth really is. All he knows is: truth = power, and rule = tyranny. We believe the lie that God's rule is tyrannical and then we choose to rule in the same way.

⊖ apply

6. Can you think of examples of truth getting twisted by political and economic interests?

⊕ investigate

"Truth = power and rule = tyranny." But the kingdom of Jesus isn't like the kingdoms of this world. Jesus is a very different sort of King.

7. Who is innocent and who is guilty (v 39-40)? Who will die in the place of the other?

8. What does this suggest about what it means for Jesus to be King?

▶ Read John 19 v 1-6

9. "Here is the man!" God's King is publicly presented. What does humanity make of Him?

▶ Read John 19 v 7-11

10. Pilate believes might is right. What's the reality?

▶ Read John 19 v 12-16

This is where human power takes us: the truth gets so twisted that Pilate condemns a man he knows to be innocent and the Jews swear allegiance to a lord they hate.

⊡ **explore more**

optional

▶ Read John 12 v 31-33

What is the judgment that takes place during the trial of Jesus? How does Jesus exercise His reign as King?

⊟ **apply**

11. What is the good news in a world of oppression, manipulation and spin?

12. Satan portrayed God as a tyrant. What is the truth about God's rule?

⊡ getting personal

How do you use authority in work, home, church and the community? Does your authority reflect the lie of Satan? Or does your authority reflect the truth about God's rule?

⬆ pray

Pray that our politicians and leaders would use their authority for good and value truth.

Pray that your life, and especially your use of authority, might show people that it is good to live under God's reign.

7 A DEMANDING SCEPTIC

⊕ talkabout

1. What do you make of this quote? *"Every faith in the world is based on fabrication. That is the definition of faith—acceptance of that which we can imagine to be true, that which we cannot prove. Every religion describes God through metaphor, allegory and exaggeration. Those who truly understand their faiths understand the stories are metaphorical."*

⊥ investigate

Jesus had been dead for two days. But that morning, Mary Magdalene returned from His tomb and told His disciples she had seen and spoken with Him.

> **Read John 20 v 19-26**

2. Does Thomas want to believe that Jesus is alive, do you think?

3. Does Thomas think that the disciples' talk of resurrection is a metaphor, do you think?

❯ Read John 20 v 27-31

4. What does Jesus offer Thomas?

5. What does Jesus command Thomas?

6. What is the message of the Gospel of John?

7. Where have we seen this message before?

8. We cannot touch Jesus as Thomas did. What evidence can we base our faith on (v 31)?

 explore more

❯ Read 1 John 1 v 1-4

What parallels are there with the story of Thomas?

optional

⊟ apply

9. How would Thomas respond to the quote in Question One, do you think?

10. Is it true that "seeing is believing"?

People don't believe because they don't like the implications of belief. They don't want to say: "My Lord and my God". They want to say: "I am my lord and I am my god".

In 14 v 5-7 Jesus tells Thomas that to see Him is to see God. It would be an outrageous claim were it not for the fact that Jesus has been raised by God from the dead. Thomas realises the implication: we must serve Jesus as our Lord and God.

This story suggests other implications of believing in the resurrection of Jesus.

11. What do verses 19, 21 and 26 all have in common? What is the implication for us?

12. What are the implications spelled out in verses 21-23?

⊕ investigate

13. What is the promise of verse 31?

Jesus may not be visible on earth any more. But He is present through the words of His disciples and the work of His Spirit. And He says: "Stop doubting and believe". He invites us to find life in His name. Our response must be: "My Lord and my God".

⊡ getting personal

How will you make sure you remember the experience of Thomas next time you are sneered at for believing in the resurrection?
Who do you know who you could tell the story of Thomas to in order to encourage them to see that Christian faith is neither blind nor dumb?

⊕ pray

What is it about Jesus and His provision for you that you find hard to hold on to? Pray that you will stop doubting and believe.

What is it about Jesus and His lordship over you that you find it hard to obey? Pray that you will cry: "My Lord and my God".

Introducing
Jesus
LEADER'S GUIDE

Leader's Guide

INTRODUCTION

Leading a Bible study can be a bit like herding cats—everyone has a different idea of what the passage could be about, and a different line of enquiry that they want to pursue. But a good group leader is more than someone who just referees this kind of discussion. You will want to:

• correctly understand and handle the Bible passage. But also…

• encourage and train the people in your group to do this for themselves. Don't fall into the trap of spoon-feeding people by simply passing on the information in the Leader's Guide. Then…

• make sure that no Bible study is finished without everyone knowing how the passage is relevant for them. What changes do you all need to make in the light of the things you have been learning? And finally…

• encourage the group to turn all that has been learned and discussed into prayer.

Your Bible-study group is unique, and you are likely to know better than anyone the capabilities, backgrounds and circumstances of the people you are leading. That's why we've designed these guides with a number of optional features. If they're a quiet bunch, you might want to spend longer on talkabout. If your time is limited, you can choose to skip explore more, or get people to look at these questions at home. Can't get enough of Bible study? Well, some studies have optional extra homework projects. As leader, you can adapt and select the material to the needs of your particular group.

So what's in the Leader's Guide?
The main thing that this Leader's Guide will help you to do is to understand the major teaching points in the passage you are studying, and how to apply them. As well as guidance on the questions, the Leader's Guide for each session contains the following important sections:

THE BIG IDEA

One key sentence will give you the main point of the session. This is what you should be aiming to have fixed in people's minds as they leave the Bible study. And it's the point you need to head back towards when the discussion goes off at a tangent.

SUMMARY

An overview of the passage, including plenty of useful historical background information.

OPTIONAL EXTRA

Usually this is an introductory activity that ties in with the main theme of the Bible study, and is designed to "break the ice" at the beginning of a session. Or it may be a "homework project" that people can tackle during the week.

So let's take a look at the various different features of a Good Book Guide:

⊕ talkabout

Each session kicks off with a discussion question, based on the group's opinions or experiences. It's designed to get people talking and thinking in a general way about the main subject of the Bible study.

⬇ investigate

The first thing you and your group need to know is what the Bible passage is about, which is the purpose of these questions. But watch out—people may come up with answers based on their experiences or teaching they have heard in the past, without referring to the passage at all. It's amazing how often we can get through a Bible study without actually looking at the Bible! If you're stuck for an answer, the Leader's Guide contains guidance on questions. These are the answers to direct your group to. This information isn't meant to be read out to people—ideally, you want them to discover these answers from the Bible for themselves. Sometimes there are optional follow-up questions (see ☑ in guidance on questions) to help you help your group get to the answer.

⊡ explore more

These questions generally point people to other relevant parts of the Bible. They are useful for helping your group to see how the passage fits into the "big picture" of the whole Bible. These sections are OPTIONAL—only use them if you have time. Remember that it's better to finish in good time having really grasped one big thing from the passage, than to try and cram everything in.

⮕ apply

We want to encourage you to spend more time working at application—too often, it is simply tacked on at the end. In the Good Book Guides, apply sections are mixed in with the investigate sections of the study. We hope that people will realise that application is not just an optional extra, but rather, the whole purpose of studying the

Bible. We do Bible study so that our lives can be changed by what we hear from God's word. If you skip the application, the Bible study hasn't achieved its purpose.

These questions draw out practical lessons that we can all learn from the Bible passage. You can review what has been learned so far, and think about practical differences that this should make in our churches and our lives. The group gets the opportunity to talk about what they personally have learned.

⬇ getting personal

These can be done at home, but it is well worth allowing a few moments of quiet reflection during the study for each person to think and pray about specific changes they need to make in their own lives. Why not have a time for reporting back at the beginning of the following session, so that everyone can be encouraged and challenged by one another to make application a priority?

⬆ pray

In Acts 4 v 25-30 the first Christians quoted Psalm 2 as they prayed in response to the persecution of the apostles by the Jewish religious leaders. Today however, it's not as common for Christians to base prayers on the truths of God's word as it once was. As a result, our prayers tend to be weak, superficial and self-centred rather than bold, visionary and God-centred.

The prayer section is based on what has been learned from the Bible passage. How different our prayer times would be if we were genuinely responding to what God has said to us through His word.

1 John 3
A CONFUSED MINISTER

THE BIG IDEA
We need God's Spirit to enable us to recognise God's King because we hide our need for a crucified King.

SUMMARY
Verses 1-10: People need Spirit-transformation to recognise God's King. (Jesus describes this Spirit-transformation through the picture of new birth.)

Verses 10-18: The reason people need this Spirit-transformation is God's King doesn't look anything like what we expect from a king. This King is "exalted" or "lifted up" on a cross because He dies to save His people. (Jesus describes this lifting up on the cross through the picture of Moses lifting up the bronze snake so that those who looked at it could be healed of God's plague of judgment.)

Verses 19-21: The underlying reason people don't recognise the crucified King is what the cross reveals about humanity: that we are evil people who need a Saviour. People will not admit their need nor submit their lives. (Jesus describes this refusal to accept His salvation through the picture of light and darkness—people prefer to hide in darkness.)

OPTIONAL EXTRA
Play a game in which volunteers are blindfolded and invited to identify objects through touch alone. Depending on who is playing, you could increase the "yuck" factor as you go along (introducing objects like mashed-up banana). This introduces the ideas of 3 v 19-21—that we need to come into the light to see and know God.

GUIDANCE ON QUESTIONS
1. What reasons do people give for ignoring or rejecting Jesus? There are many possible answers to this question. What we will see in this study is that behind all these reasons is the big reason that people don't want to admit their need or submit to Jesus. But let this truth unfold as you look at the passage together.

2. What is the question behind the statement by Nicodemus in verse 2? The "reply" of Jesus in verse 3 does not seem a reply to the statement in verse 2 until you realise that behind the statement by Nicodemus is an implied question.

⌄

• **Who were the Jews expecting would one day come from God? What did they expect him to do?** They were expecting God's Messiah (His promised Saviour-King) to come and defeat God's enemies. So really Nicodemus is asking: Are you God's promised King? Are you bringing God's kingdom?

3. How is verse 3 a "reply" to verse 2? Behind verse 2 is the question of whether Jesus is God's King bringing God's kingdom. Verse 3 says you need to be born again to know the answer to that question. Nicodemus can't see the answer unless he is born again. Look at 2 v 23-25. Nicodemus says Jesus is from God (which implies a measure of faith) because He performs miracles ("signs", v 2). But John has just said that Jesus does not trust faith that comes simply through seeing miracles (1 v 23-24).

4. What do you need in order to see and enter God's kingdom? To be born again (v 3) = born of the Spirit (v 5-8).

• **Nicodemus is confused because he takes this literally (v 4). Being born again of the Spirit is a picture. Of what?** Of new life through the Spirit, an inner transformation that the Spirit produces in us. The Spirit enables us to recognise who Jesus is and gives us a new desire to serve Him. Theologians call this "regeneration", which means "rebirth".

Jesus says you must be born "of water and the Spirit" (v 5). People may ask what is meant by "of water". It is probably a reference to baptism. Baptism is the outward sign of the Spirit's inward transformation. In John 1 v 29-34 John baptises with water "that [Jesus] might be revealed to Israel", but Jesus baptises with the Holy Spirit = gives inward change and insight through the Spirit.

EXPLORE MORE
Read Ezekiel 36 v 25-27. How does the promise in Ezekiel match the words of Jesus to Nicodemus? How will the promise in Ezekiel be fulfilled?
The people of Israel need a change of heart to know God, to treasure Him and to serve Him. Jesus says we need Spirit-transformation to see and enter God's kingdom. The Spirit will do this work in people's lives as a result of the saving work of Jesus.

5. APPLY: What does "born again" mean in our society? A "born-again Christian" has largely negative connotations in our culture. It usually means either an uncool or fanatical Christian.

6. APPLY: What does Jesus mean by being "born again"? Jesus says you cannot see or enter God's kingdom without being born again. So all Christians are born-again Christians. It means people who have been enlightened and changed by the Holy Spirit.

7. Nicodemus is part of the political and religious establishment. What do you think he might expect God's King to be like? In verse 1 we are told that Nicodemus is a Pharisee and a member of the Jewish ruling council. As a member of the religious elite, he probably expected God's Messiah to be a holy prophet blessed by God. As part of the political establishment, he probably expected God's king to be a powerful man, leading a conquering army.

8. We expect a king to be exalted— "lifted up". And God's King will be "lifted up". But what does Jesus actually mean? (See John 12 v 32-33.) Jesus is talking about being lifted up on the cross. This is why people can't see God's kingdom without the work of God's Spirit—God's King doesn't look anything like what we might expect.

9. Turn to Numbers 21 v 6-9 to discover the background to verse 14. Why will God's King be exalted or "lifted up" on a cross? Just as people were saved when they looked at the snake lifted up on the pole, so people will be saved when they trust in Jesus lifted up on the cross (v 15-17). Jesus has not come as God's King to condemn God's enemies (though one day He will). If He had come in this way, we would all be condemned because we are all God's enemies. Instead Jesus is condemned in our place on the cross so that we might be saved.

10. What must we do to be saved by God's King? We are saved through believing in Jesus. Ask people where we see this in the passage so that they see it is repeated in verses 15, 16, and 18. You could first ask how a religious person might answer this question? How would "Nick the Vic" have answered it before he met Jesus? You might also want to highlight that believing in Jesus is related to seeing who Jesus is, and this seeing is the Spirit's work (v 3-8). This means faith is God's gift to us through the Spirit.

11. See 1 v 1-9. When did God's light come into the world? God's light came into the world in the person of Jesus. In other words, Jesus is the light (8 v 12). Jesus reveals the truth about God.

12. What stops people "seeing" and coming into God's kingdom? First, people love darkness (3 v 19) = they don't want to let go of their sin and submit to Jesus. Second, people fear exposure (v 20) = they don't what to acknowledge their sin and admit their need of a Saviour.

13. When does this conversation take place and why? Look back at verse 2. Nicodemus comes to Jesus at night, probably because he doesn't want people to know he's meeting Jesus.

14. How does Jesus interpret the setting that Nicodemus chose for his chat with Jesus? Nicodemus comes to Jesus by night because he fears exposure. He doesn't want

to admit his interest in Jesus. Jesus says all people are like that: we don't want to admit our need of Jesus. We prefer to walk in darkness than to be exposed by the light.

15. APPLY: What does this conversation suggest Christians must do if they want to know God better? We need to come into the light (v 21). We need to confess our sin rather than hide in darkness. We need repeatedly to expose our sin to the light of God and His word. See Psalm 32.

16. APPLY: What are the implications for our evangelism? We can't give people new birth or enable them to see Jesus. This is the Spirit's work. This means there's no point in being manipulative or pressurising people. Our role is to set out the truth about Jesus plainly and pray that God will open the minds of people through the Spirit to see the glory of Jesus. See 2 Corinthians 4 v 1–6.

2 John 4
A DESPERATE WOMAN

THE BIG IDEA
Our lives are driven by a desire for satisfaction and meaning which only Jesus can meet in a true and lasting way.

SUMMARY
Verses 1-14: Jesus meets a Samaritan woman at a well and offers her "living water" (though she is confused because she thinks he is talking literally about physical water). In 7 v 37-39 John says "living water" is a picture of the Holy Spirit. Through the gift of the Holy Spirit we can have a relationship with God that quenches our spiritual thirst—ie: brings satisfaction, meaning and fulfilment.

Verses 15-18: Jesus appears to change the subject when He asks about the woman's husband. In fact He is exposing where this woman currently looks for satisfaction, meaning and fulfilment—through a series of sexual relationships. But the maths tells the story: she has sought from a man what only God can give in a true and lasting way. As a result she has gone from one man to another.

Verses 19-24: This time the woman changes the subject. She asks where worship should take place. But once again Jesus uses this to go to the heart of the issue. True worship is not a matter of "where?" but "what?" The woman values men as the source of meaning and satisfaction. But true worship is to value God above all else.

Verses 25-42: The woman goes to the well at noon (v 6). But normally people do not collect water at the hottest time of day. She does so to avoid the other women

of the village because of her shame. But after meeting the Messiah she goes back to the village and says: "Come, see a man who told me everything I've ever done"—a testimony that brings the other villagers to Jesus.

Verses 31-38: Just as Jesus offers the woman living water, He says that He has (spiritual) food = to do God's will. He "shares" this food with His disciples as He calls them to mission.

OPTIONAL EXTRA
Bring a variety of magazines and ask people to look at the adverts. With what longings are these adverts aiming to connect?

GUIDANCE ON QUESTIONS
1. Think of things that people look to for satisfaction and identity. Answers could include things like possessions, status, sex, relationships, hobbies, children and so on.

2. Why is this woman surprised when Jesus asks her for a drink? See verse 9. John fills in the background for us. The Jews did not associate with the Samaritans because they practised a disputed form of Judaism and they were not ethnically pure. Not only is she a Samaritan, but she is a woman, and Jewish men did not treat women as equals.

3. Why is this woman surprised when Jesus offers her a drink? See verse 11. She is standing by a well with a bucket. Jesus is standing by a well with no bucket. It looks as if she's the only one who's going to be providing water. But she has misunderstand the offer of Jesus. She has taken his picture language literally (just as Nicodemus did in 3 v 4 and 12).

4. How does Jesus explain His offer of a drink in verses 13-14? Jesus is not offering literal, physical water, which only quenches our thirst temporarily. He is using water as a picture (that's why he refers to it as "living water" in v 10). He is pointing to a reality that satisfies for ever (you "will never thirst" and "welling up to eternal life").

5. Look at 7 v 37-39. What is the reality that Jesus pictures as "living water"? John tells us that the living water comes through the Holy Spirit. We were made to know God and that's how we find true satisfaction. The Holy Spirit is God in us and the Spirit unites us to Christ so that we have a relationship with the triune God.

6. How has this woman been trying to satisfy her spiritual thirst? She has been trying to find satisfaction and identity in sexual relationships and intimacy. Some people have such a strong desire to be loved that they are prepared to "buy" it with sex. Others have a strong desire to be desired— in effect, to be worshipped.

7. How do we know that this has not brought true and lasting joy? Look at verse 18. She has been trying to find satisfaction and identity from a man instead of from God. In the process she has made an idol of sexual intimacy. But it has not brought satisfaction and so she is left moving from one man to another.

8. APPLY: Look back at your answers to Q1. Many of these things do provide a measure of satisfaction and identity. But evaluate where they lie on a line between partial and full satisfaction, and a line between temporary and lasting satisfaction. People in your group will put different things in different places! But none of them will give full, lasting satisfaction (unless someone said "Jesus" in Q1!)

9. What does the woman think true worship comes down to? A matter of location. So she asks whether worship should take place on this mountain (= Mount Gerizim in Samaritan territory) or in Jerusalem.

10. How does Jesus define true worship? As a matter of the heart. It's about what your heart desires (worship in spirit) and what you think will truly satisfy (worship in truth). If we sing about God's goodness, but treasure other things above Him, then we are not worshipping in truth! Whenever we look to God for identity, meaning and fulfilment, we declare His worth (His "worth-ship") in our lives. We worship Jesus as we treasure Jesus, counting Him more worthy than anything else. See Matthew 13 v 44-46.

11. Look back at verses 6-7. Women collected water in the early morning while it was still cool. Why do you think this woman collects water at the hottest time of the day? The fact that John draws attention to the time of day suggests it is significant. This woman wants to avoid meeting the other women of the village. She lives with a strong sense of shame. She knows they gossip about her. Maybe they jostle her if she comes to the well when they do.

12. Look at verse 29. What does she do after meeting the Messiah? She goes to the people she has been avoiding. And she invites them to meet "a man who told me everything I've ever done". Meeting Jesus has removed her shame. Her reputation is no longer a big deal. She is too excited about the Messiah. John also tells us that she left her water jar. Perhaps he intends this as a picture of her new life. She is no longer looking for water in the way she did before.

13. Look at verse 39. What is it that causes the Samaritans to believe in Jesus? Although their faith is strengthened as they get to know Jesus (v 42), they initially believe because of the woman's invitation to meet a man who "told me everything I've ever done". Her confession of sin and her shame-free testimony lead others to Jesus.

14. APPLY: What lessons are there for our evangelism? We can all tell the story of what Jesus has done for us and this is a powerful testimony to Him. We don't

witness to our good works, nor do we have to pretend we (or our church) are wonderful. We can be honest and real with people because we point to a gracious Saviour and His gracious invitation to find true satisfaction in Him. The way Jesus takes away our shame is more powerful than any pretence at self-righteousness!

EXPLORE MORE
Read John 4 v 31-38. What are the parallels between this conversation and the conversation between Jesus and the woman? What food does Jesus have to satisfy His spiritual appetite? What invitation does He give to His disciples? Both conversations appear to be about satisfying your appetite (thirst and hunger). But in both cases Jesus is using water and food as a picture of spiritual satisfaction. Doing God's will is like feasting on spiritual food. And Jesus invites us to share the feast: to find joy working for a spiritual harvest.

3 John 6
A NEEDY CROWD

THE BIG IDEA
Jesus truly satisfies our needs, but He only satisfies our true needs.

SUMMARY
Jesus feeds 5,000 men and says that this is a sign or pointer to His identity = He is "the bread of life". As with the offer of "living water" in John 4, He satisfies our spiritual hunger and thirst (6 v 35).

In verses 22-34 the crowd come to Jesus looking for satisfaction. But they don't want to find satisfaction in Him. They aren't looking for a relationship with God. They simply want Jesus to provide bread. Like many people, they look to Jesus to provide, but they want Him to meet their selfish desires.

Verses 35-59: The crowd cannot see beyond their immediate desires to recognise the true life that is found in Jesus. Jesus offers spiritual life now, resurrection on the last day and eternal life to those who believe in Him.

Jesus can give life to His people because He gives His life for His people (v 51). When you live for something other than God and you don't measure up, it will crush you (leave you angry, depressed or bitter). When you live for God and you don't measure up, He is crushed for you. Jesus gave His life for your life so that you can receive eternal life.

OPTIONAL EXTRA

Serve warm, freshly baked bread and talk together about its properties.

GUIDANCE ON QUESTIONS

1. Have you ever known someone get angry with God because God didn't give them what they wanted? People may want to talk about their own experience, but this question is phrased so that this is not required of them. As people tell their stories, they may offer some analysis of why God didn't "deliver". There is no need to comment on this at this stage. Instead let the passage provide a commentary as you look at it together.

2. John often presents a miracle of Jesus together with some teaching of Jesus so that the teaching explains the miracle. How does verse 35 explain the miraculous feeding of 5,000 men? The feeding of 5,000 men is a picture and proof of the claim that Jesus can satisfy us eternally.

3. Why do the crowd come looking for Jesus? The crowd want to eat their fill of bread. They aren't interested in the miraculous signs and the true identity of Jesus to which these signs point.

4. What does Jesus offer instead? Food that "endures to eternal life". He offers "enduring food" = true and lasting satisfaction (just as He offered the woman at the well "living water" = true and lasting satisfaction).

5. What does the crowd ask for? It doesn't look as if Jesus is going to give them more bread, so they try a different approach. Jesus has said they should pay more attention to the miraculous signs and what they point to. So they ask for a sign—a sign like the one Moses gave of bread from heaven. In other words, they are just asking for bread again, albeit dressed up in pious-sounding language!

6. How does Jesus respond? Look at verse 32. The crowd are focusing on the gift (and its means of delivery = Moses) instead of focusing on the Giver (= the Father in heaven). Look at verse 33. The crowd are focusing on physical bread instead of focusing on living bread (= the One who comes from heaven). In other words, just as the crowd is asking for physical bread again, so Jesus is offering spiritual bread again.

7. What is it is that truly satisfies us eternally? Look at verse 35. It is Jesus Himself who truly satisfies. He doesn't just provide satisfaction; He is satisfaction. He doesn't provide the good life; He is the good life. As Augustine prayed: "Our hearts are restless until they find their rest in you".

8. How do we receive true satisfaction? Look at verses 28-29, 35-36 and 40. We receive the bread of life through faith. If we come to Jesus and believe in Jesus, we will never be spiritually hungry or thirsty again. This refers to becoming a Christian—we become a Christian by believing in Jesus.

But it also describes how, as Christians, we continue to be satisfied in God. We are satisfied in God as we affirm through faith that He is the true source of eternal joy and as we delight in His glory through faith.

9. APPLY: What's wrong with looking to Jesus to satisfy you in the way that the crowd did? We should look to Jesus to satisfy us, but we should look to Him to satisfy us with Himself. He doesn't promise to satisfy our needs however we define them. Jesus doesn't simply meet our desires. He radically reshapes those desires.

10. APPLY: What's wrong with wanting bread? Nothing! Sinful desires are not always, or even often, desires for wrong things. They are desires that have grown bigger to us than our desire for God. The crowd were more interested in bread than in Jesus.

11. APPLY: The crowd ask for bread in verse 31 with a quote from the Bible. Can you think of examples of people today dressing up selfish desires with pious language? The so-called "prosperity gospel" is a large-scale example in which people promise that God will give health, wealth and success. See if you can also identify examples in your own experience.

12. What happens to those who believe Jesus is the bread of life? They receive eternal life. See verses 39, 40, 44, 47, 50, 51. They will face physical death at the end of their lives, but Jesus will raise them up on the last day to live eternally.

13. Why does Jesus say the living bread is His flesh? Jesus is not speaking literally about some kind of cannibalism! Once again, people mistake His picture language

(3 v 4, 12; 4 v 15; 6 v 52). Jesus is talking about His death. He's not talking about believing in some ideal or in a body of teaching. He's talking about believing in a real flesh-and-blood person who offers His body "for the life of the world" (v 51).

14. APPLY: If you live for something other than God, what happens when you don't measure up? If, for example, you live for possessions, what happens when you lose your job? If you live for marriage, what happens if you can't find a spouse or your spouse is adulterous? If you live for control, what happens when things go wrong? The answer is that your "idol" crushes you. You're left feeling angry or depressed or bitter.

15. APPLY: If you live for God, what happens when you don't measure up? If you live for an idol, you are crushed when you don't measure up. But if you live for God, He is crushed when you don't measure up. Jesus gave His life for your life so that you can receive eternal life.

4 John 9
A LIFELONG LOSER

THE BIG IDEA

Jesus displays His glory in the least likely people, which means self-important people don't see who He is.

SUMMARY

Jesus and the disciples see a man blind from birth. The disciples assume he must have been cursed by God. But he has been blind from birth—before he could have committed a sin. So did he sin in the womb? Did God curse him ahead of time for a future sin he would one day commit? Or did his parents sin? They're confused!

Jesus says the man is not blind as a judgment against some specific sin (though suffering is the result of God's curse against humanity's sin in general). This man was born blind so that God might be glorified in his life. Suffering has a purpose and that purpose is God's glory. Those society thinks of as "losers" are often used by God to display His grace and glory.

After Jesus heals the man, the Pharisees investigate the healing. As the conversations progress we see the Pharisees hardening in their rejection of Jesus—they become blind to the truth. Meanwhile the man increasingly realises who Jesus really is—he comes to see the truth. He starts to use sarcasm to highlight the blindness of the Pharisees. He realises they don't want to "see" Jesus because they do not want to follow Jesus (see also 3 v 19-21).

Jesus provides an interpretation of this in 9 v 39: "For judgment I have come into this world, so that the blind will see and those who see will become blind."

OPTIONAL EXTRA

Ask people to flick through some celebrity magazines. What do the magazines regard as important? How do the magazines evaluate people?

GUIDANCE ON QUESTIONS

1. Who does our society regard as "losers"? Keep this general—not about individuals!

2. Why did the disciples think the blind man was a "loser"? The disciples believed this blind man had been cursed by God. They thought blindness was a direct judgment for some specific sin. What confused them was that, since this man was blind from birth, it was difficult to know how his blindness could be a curse for sin. So they speculated that he might have been cursed for a sin of his parents. See also v 34.

3. Why did Jesus say the man was blind? Jesus says this man is not blind because of judgment against some specific sin (though sickness and suffering are the result of God's curse against humanity's sin in a general sense). Instead this man was born blind so that God might be glorified in his life.

4. Look at verses 4-5. What is the day and night to which Jesus refers? Before electric light bulbs no work could be done after dark. Verse 5 suggests Jesus is referring to His time on earth, with the night referring to the cross. (See 12 v 30-36. Also the "night" in 13 v 30 may be a picture of time of the cross.) But the invitation for the disciples to do God's work in the day in

9 v 4 suggests Jesus is referring to the mission of the church, with the night representing the final judgment.

5. How do the events of verses 6-12 explain and prove the claim of Jesus in verse 5? Jesus claims to be the light of the world. See also 1 v 1-13 and 8 v 12. In this story He enables a man to see. Jesus calls Himself the light because He enables us to see God. The healing of a blind man is a picture of His ability to bring spiritual enlightenment to our spiritual confusion and darkness.

6. APPLY: Look at 9 v 3 and 11 v 4. What do these stories show is one purpose of suffering in our lives? God uses suffering in our lives to display His work and glorify His name.

7. APPLY: How should this purpose change the way we suffer? We should see our suffering as an opportunity to glorify God.

⊗

• **How can we glorify God through our suffering?** By praising Christ in the midst of suffering we show that He is more valuable than what we have lost. See also 2 Corinthians 1 v 3-7.

EXPLORE MORE
Read 1 Corinthians 1 v 26-31. Who does God choose? Why does God choose them? He chooses "losers"—the foolish, weak and lowly people of this world. He does this so that He might display His grace. No one is able to say: "I was saved because of my intellect, power or influence". In this way God shames those who proudly prize their intellect, power and influence.

You might want to assess whether Paul's description of God's people matches your church and, if not, why not.

8. What is the Pharisees' attitude to this healing and to Jesus? How does it change during their conversation with the man born blind? It might help to focus on these "turning points": verses 16, 18, 22, 24, 27-28, 34. At first the Pharisees appear genuinely to debate the identity of Jesus (v 13-16). But they are reluctant to come to the conclusion that Jesus is a prophet (v 17-18). The man's parents stick to facts without offering interpretation because they understand that the Pharisees have already prejudged the issue (v 18-23). Their prejudice is revealed in verse 24 and its reason is revealed in their violent reaction to the man's question in verse 27: they do not want to follow Jesus. (On their claim to be disciples of Moses, see 5 v 46-47.)

9. Highlight moments of humour in this conversation. The reactions of the man born blind increasingly highlight in a sarcastic way the blindness of the Pharisees. Read in the right way, the humour is very clear. "We know," they confidently assert in verse 24. "I don't know," the man says in response, but then states facts that refute their claim to know: "One thing I do know. I was blind but now I see!" Verse 27 again highlights their inability to "see it". The man born blind asks: "Do you want to become his disciples too?" but almost certainly realises their reactions are caused by their unwillingness to follow Jesus. In verse 30 his sarcasm is clear: "Now that is remarkable!" Again he highlights how their claims to know don't match any of the facts.

10. How does the understanding of the man born blind develop during the

story? It might help to focus on the ways in which he describes Jesus in verses 11, 17, 33 and 38. At first the man born blind describes Jesus as "the man they call Jesus" (v 11). His understanding of Jesus is basic and secondhand. But the conversations with the Pharisees begin to clarify in his mind who Jesus must be. He concludes He must be a prophet (v 17) and a man from God (v 33) because of what He has done. But after his conversation with Jesus, he worships Jesus as Lord (v 38).

11. Look at verse 39. How do these words of Jesus provide a commentary on the story? The story is the story of a man who is physically blind, but who comes to see who Jesus is. And it is the story of religious leaders who can physically see, but who reveal themselves to be spiritually blind. It is the coming of Jesus that forces the issue for everyone. The way that people respond to Jesus reveals their hearts and forms the basis of their future judgment by God.

12. What is the meaning of verse 41? Verse 41 parallels the ideas of Mark 2 v 17. Those who claim they have understanding are confident in themselves. But in fact human beings are all corrupt and spiritually blind. We cannot enlighten or save ourselves. Our only hope is to recognise we are blind and look to Jesus to show us the way (John 14 v 6).

13. APPLY: What are the implications of this story for the way we read the Bible? See Isaiah 66 v 1-2. The Pharisees thought they already knew all about God so they dramatically missed all the evidence. Because they thought they could see, they didn't look to Jesus for insight (John 9 v 41). We should approach God's word humbly, without assuming we already know all about

God, and ask God to give us understanding. The reason the Pharisees cannot see Jesus is that they do not want to follow Him (v 27-28). We need to approach the Bible with a willingness to submit to its teachings and as part of a community that will encourage us to live in obedience to God's word.

14. APPLY: What does verse 39 suggest happens when we tell people about Jesus? See also 2 Corinthians 2 v 15-16. When we speak to people about Jesus, judgment takes place. The way that people respond to the message of Jesus reveals their hearts and forms the basis of their future judgment by God.

15. APPLY: Who are the real "losers" in this story? How might this change the way we view other people? At the beginning of the story it looks as if the man who has been blind from birth is the "loser", but by the end it is clear that the Pharisees are the real "losers". We are often impressed by looks, intellect, power or performance. We dismiss people who don't measure up to these standards as "losers". But this story shows that a person's attitude to Jesus is what really matters. God is more often glorified through people this world regards as "losers".

5

John 11
A GRIEVING FAMILY

THE BIG IDEA
Jesus offers genuine comfort in the face of death, sharing our pain and offering real hope.

SUMMARY
Martha and Mary both greet Jesus after the death of their brother with exactly the same words (v 21 and 32). But Jesus responds very differently. He doesn't offer a one-size-fits-all response to suffering. He responds to people in a way that fits their needs and personalities.

Martha expresses strong faith in resurrection. But Jesus personalises this faith: He is the resurrection and the life. In Jesus we will be raised again after death and in Jesus we can experience spiritual life now.

In response to Mary, Jesus says nothing. He simply weeps with her, expressing His sorrow and anger at the effects of sin in the world.

Jesus offers more than comforting words and sympathetic tears. He offers genuine hope because He has power over life and death. He demonstrates this by bringing Lazarus back from the dead.

OPTIONAL EXTRA
In connection with Q1, show an extract from a film which depicts someone responding to death or bereavement. Ask people what they would say to the person in the film. Possible films include *Stepmom* or *Cold Mountain*.

GUIDANCE ON QUESTIONS
1. What would you say to someone
who has recently been bereaved? If you have someone in the group who has fairly recently been bereaved, then you could ask them beforehand if they would be willing to talk about what they would have liked people to do or say.

2. What are the similarities in these verses with the story of the man born blind in John 9 (who we looked at in the last session)? Compare 9 v 3 and 11 v 4. In both stories, adversity becomes an opportunity for God to be glorified (see 11 v 15). Compare also 9 v 4-5 and 11 v 9-10.

☒

- **What do 9 v 4-5 and 11 v 9-10 mean for Jesus?** In 11 v 7-8 the disciples ask why Jesus is going to Judea when this means risking death. Jesus says He must complete His Father's work while it is still day (before His death).
- **What do these verses mean for the disciples?** Jesus' death will only come at the appointed time. The disciples, too, must learn to do God's work while they have the opportunity and before judgment comes.

3. Look at verses 21-24. What do Martha's words reveal about her faith? Martha expresses strong faith. She believes in the power of Jesus to heal. She believes He has power to change the situation though she does not appear to expect Jesus to raise Lazarus from the dead immediately because that is not how she interprets Jesus' statement in verse 23. Not all Jews at that time believed in life after death (Mark 12 v 18). But Martha shares the fullest and highest expression of Jewish faith in resurrection.

4. Look at verses 25-26. What does Jesus add to her faith in resurrection?

Jesus adds Himself to Martha's faith in resurrection. He invites Martha not only to believe in the concept of resurrection, but to see Him as its source and foundation.

5. What does Jesus mean when He calls Himself "the resurrection and the life", do you think?

⮟

• If your group are struggling, you could ask: Does Jesus mean two related, but different things by "resurrection" and "life" or is He reiterating the same point? How do the rest of verses 25-26 explain the claim of Jesus to be the resurrection and the life?

Jesus is saying that He is the source and grounds of the resurrection. The rest of verses 25-26 explain what He means. (1) "I am the resurrection" = "the one who believes in me will live, even though they dies". In other words, Christians will experience physical death, but Jesus will raise us up again to life after death. (2) "I am ... the life" = "whoever lives by believing in me will never die". In other words, Christians already experience spiritual life or eternal life and will always do so (even though they experience physical death).

6. What response does Jesus look for?

Jesus asks Martha: "Do you believe this?" He invites her to put her faith in Him as the resurrection and life. In verse 24 she believes in the idea of resurrection. But as a result of her conversation with Jesus she believes in the person of Jesus.

EXPLORE MORE
Read John 3 v 16, 36; 5 v 24-29; 6 v 47-51; 12 v 23-25. How do these passages reinforce what Jesus says to Martha? What do they add to what Jesus says to Martha? These passages reinforce the idea that resurrection and eternal life come through believing in Jesus, and that Jesus has been given authority to give life. They add the idea that those who reject Jesus will perish or experience eternal death. They also suggest how it is that Jesus gives life. He gives life by laying down His own life (6 v 51; 12 v 24). Jesus takes the penalty of death that we deserve for our sin so that we don't have to. In a follow-up to the story of Lazarus being raised from the dead, Caiaphas, the high priest, unwittingly expresses this same truth—see verses 49-50.

7. APPLY: Martha expresses her confidence in Jesus before He has raised Lazarus from the dead. Look at v 45-48. The Jewish leaders reject Jesus after they hear of the raising of Lazarus. What does this teach us about true faith? True faith continues to trust in Jesus even when we suffer or are bereaved. It is not just faith for the good times. See also 2 v 18-25. The disciples come to true faith through the Scriptures and words of Jesus. In contrast, Jesus does not trust faith that comes through miracles because such faith may only last as long as things are going well.

8. How does Jesus respond to Mary?

Jesus sees the tears of Mary and is "deeply moved in spirit and troubled". He responds to tears with tears.

9. What does Jesus reveal about God's response to bereavement and death? God is not indifferent or apathetic about our suffering. He has compassion on His people. He shares our grief. Indeed God the Father has experienced bereavement and God the Son has experienced death. See Hebrews 4 v 14-16. The word translated "deeply moved" implies anger. God is angry that death has entered His good world. Death is a scandalous outrage.

10. Compare verses 21 and 32. Martha and Mary both greet Jesus with exactly the same words. But Jesus responds very differently. Why do you think this is? Martha and Mary were different people with different personalities and so Jesus responded to them in different ways.

11. APPLY: What lessons are there for us when we meet bereaved people? We shouldn't try to give a one-size-fits-all response to bereavement and suffering. Some people have genuine questions with which we need to wrestle. With other people we will just cry together. We also need to cry with God: we need to grieve over a world wrecked by sin just as God does (see Luke 19 v 41-42).

12. APPLY: Can you think of empty words that we say when people die that do not offer any real comfort? Examples might include things like "He had a good, long life" or "Time is a great healer".

13. Why does Jesus pray out loud? John 5 v 26 says the Father has granted the Son authority over death. So Jesus wants people to realise that Lazarus will come back to life after four days because of His authority. At stake is not just whether someone can rise from the dead, but also who Jesus is.

14. John 12 v 17-18 describes the raising of Lazarus as a "sign". What does it point to? The raising of Lazarus is a sign that Jesus really is the resurrection and the life. He demonstrates that He has power over life and death. The raising of Lazarus is a promise that He will raise His people up on the last day.

EXPLORE MORE
Read 12 v 1-3. How do Martha and Mary respond to the gift of life that Jesus gives? What does this show about how we should respond to Jesus today? Martha responds by serving Jesus and showing hospitality to His people. Mary responds with extravagant love and worship.

6 John 18 – 19
AN ANXIOUS POLITICIAN

THE BIG IDEA

Jesus is not like self-serving human rulers who spin the truth. Jesus is the Servant-King, who gives His life for His people.

SUMMARY

At times the conversation between Jesus and Pilate can feel like two different conversations going on at the same time. Their responses do not always seem to follow from one another.

But we need to realise that Pilate and Jesus have completely different understandings of what it means to be a king. When Pilate asks if Jesus is a king, Jesus can't reply "yes" or "no" without being misleading (18 v 33-34). Yes, He is a king; but, no, He isn't a king in the way that Pilate understands kingship. His kingdom is not of this world (v 36); not that it is floating away in another realm, but he doesn't reign like human rulers.

The underlying problem is that in the Garden of Eden, Satan portrayed God's rule as tyrannical. Not only does humanity believe this lie and reject God's rule, but we also rule in a way that reflects the lie rather than in a way that reflects the truth of God's rule. In other words, human rule is self-serving and human rulers twist truth to serve their purposes. As a result we think God's rule is like this and so the coming of God's rule doesn't sound like good news to us. But Jesus has come to witness to the truth about God's reign (18 v 37). He does so by showing that He is not a self-serving king, but the Servant-King, who gives His life for His people.

The Romans mock Jesus the King and the

Jews reject the Jesus the King because they don't understand what kind of a king He is (19 v 1-6). In the end Pilate condemns a man he knows to be innocent (19 v 4) and the Jews swear allegiance to a lord they hate (19 v 12-16).

The good news is that:
- there is a higher throne to which all self-serving human rulers must give an account (19 v 11).
- there is a King who is not self-serving, but who dies for His people.

OPTIONAL EXTRA

Play "the game of spin". Create some news stories or announcements. For each one, either ask someone to play the part of a government spokesperson who has to "spin" bad news into good news or ask someone to play the part of an opposition spokesperson who has to "spin" good news into bad news.

GUIDANCE ON QUESTIONS

1. What do we expect from spokespeople? They ought to be truth-tellers in our society, but instead we suspect them of spreading propaganda—half-truths and lies—to promote their political and economic interests.

- **What do we expect when politicians speak in the media? What happens to truth in political debates?**

2. What is Pilate's understanding of a king? Pilate is the Roman governor. He is the representative of Caesar. He thinks of a king as Caesar—a glorious ruler with a vast empire and a powerful army. Or Pilate thinks of a king as a political rebel against that rule, intent on revolution with a band of violent followers. In 18 v 33 Pilate may be ironic: Jesus is a homeless, peasant preacher with no army: *Are you really claiming to be a king?!*

3. Look at verse 34. Why does Jesus respond in this way? Jesus can't say "no" when Pilate asks if He is a king because He is a king. But He can't say "yes" either because He's not the kind of king that Pilate has in mind. So Jesus asks from where Pilate has got this idea. In other words: *Are you asking whether I'm a Roman-style king or a Jewish-style messiah?* In verse 35 Pilate is saying, in effect: *Do you think I'm interested in Jewish messiahs?*

4. In verse 36 Jesus answers Pilate's original question about whether He is a king, but how does He redefine what it means to be a king? Jesus says His kingdom is not like the kingdoms of this world. His followers don't constitute an army and He doesn't gain power through political force. Jesus isn't saying His kingdom exists in some non-earthly realm. He has authority over the people of this world. Instead, He's saying that His kingdom is unlike any other worldly kingdom.

5. Look at verse 37. Jesus has come to testify to the truth about God's reign. What was Satan's lie about God's reign in the Garden of Eden (Genesis 3 v 1-7)? Satan portrays God as a tyrant, out to restrict human freedom and keep us in ignorance.

6. APPLY: Can you think of examples

of truth getting twisted by political and economic interests? You might like to think of an example beforehand, to get discussion started.

7. Who is innocent and who is guilty (v 39-40)? Who will die in the place of the other? Jesus is innocent (Pilate admits as much in 18 v 38) while Barabbas is guilty. But Jesus will die in the place of Barabbas— the righteous for the unrighteous.

8. What does this suggest about what it means for Jesus to be King? Jesus is the King who dies to saves His people. We assume rule = tyranny. People use power for their own selfish ends. But Jesus uses His power to save His people. Rulers oppress those who rebel against them. Jesus dies for those who rebel against Him. See also 11 v 50: Jesus dies for His people.

9. "Here is the man!" God's King is publicly presented. What does humanity make of Him? The idea of a Servant-King who dies for His people is mocked by the Roman soldiers (19 v 3) and rejected by the Jewish people (v 6).

10. Pilate believes might is right. What's the reality? Pilate thinks he is the last word in justice (v 10). He believes the might of Roman power is the ultimate authority. But Jesus reminds him that there is a higher power to which he is accountable (v 11).

EXPLORE MORE
Read 12 v 31-33. What is the judgment that takes place during the trial of Jesus? How does Jesus exercise His reign as King? Jesus is judged by Pilate and the Jewish leaders. Humanity, as it were, judges Jesus. We reject His claim to be our King. But ultimately this judgment rebounds

on us. We reject our King and our Saviour. We demonstrate that we are rebels against God. Jesus is "exalted" or "lifted up" on the cross. He demonstrates His power as a King by freely giving up His power for the sake of His people. Now He extends His reign over the world through the mission of the church. As we proclaim the message of Christ crucified, people are drawn to Christ and enter His kingdom.

11. APPLY: What is the good news in a world of oppression, manipulation and spin? There is a greater power = God

on the throne (19 v 11). Power is not the last word, nor does it define truth. Power is accountable to God. And there's a King who serves His people and dies to save them.

12. APPLY: Satan portrayed God as a tyrant. What is the truth about God's rule? The kingdom or rule of Jesus is unlike the kingdoms of this world. Jesus is the King who dies for His people. In so doing He shows us what God's rule is really like: God's rule is a rule of freedom, justice, peace and blessing. God's rule really is good news (Mark 1 v 14-15)!

7 John 20
A DEMANDING SCEPTIC

THE BIG IDEA
We can trust the testimony of the first disciples because they were not gullible fools uninterested in evidence.

SUMMARY
People sometimes think the first disciples were gullible fools who believed in the resurrection simply because they hoped it was true. Or people believe that resurrection is just a metaphor (of, for example, new beginnings). But Thomas was a sceptic who demanded proof that Jesus was alive again (v 25). We can therefore trust the testimony of the first apostles. John writes so that we might believe and Jesus says those who believe without seeing are blessed (v 29-31).

When Thomas gets proof, he recognises that the risen Jesus is Lord and God (v 28). People often say that seeing is believing. But we have already seen in John (3 v 19-21;

9 v 39) that people don't believe in Jesus because they don't want to acknowledge Him as their Lord and God. The problem is not with the evidence for Jesus, but with the rebellion of people's hearts.

The resurrection has other implications. Jesus speaks peace to the disciples (v 19, 21, 26). He is the risen Lord, who conquers our fears and our sin. And Jesus gives us a mission (v 21-22). If people accept our message, then their sins are forgiven; if they reject it, then their sins are not forgiven (v 23).

Jesus may not be visible on earth any more. But He is present through the words of His disciples. And He says: "Stop doubting and believe" (v 27). He invites us to find life in His name (v 31). Our response must be: "My Lord and my God" (v 28).

GUIDANCE ON QUESTIONS
1. What do you make of this quote?...

The quote is from Dan Brown's *The Da Vinci Code*. The aim is not only to disagree, but to work out *why* the quote is incorrect.

2. Does Thomas want to believe that Jesus is alive? He may well want to believe Jesus is alive, but he is not willing to believe without evidence. Often we rather arrogantly think ancient people were naïve and gullible compared to modern, scientific people. But Thomas is not naïve or gullible. He is not so desperate for it to be true that he will believe without evidence.

⌄

• **What does Thomas want?** He wants proof. He is a sceptic demanding evidence.

3. Does Thomas think that the disciples' talk of resurrection is a metaphor, do you think? The disciples are not talking about resurrection as a metaphor (of, for example, new beginnings). They are talking about a real person whom Thomas can demand to touch.

4. What does Jesus offer Thomas? The evidence that he seeks.

5. What does Jesus command Thomas? Look at v 27: "Stop doubting and believe."

6. What is the message of the Gospel of John? V 31: "These [things] are written that you may believe that Jesus is the Messiah, the Son of God, and that by believing you may have life in his name." Make sure people link the answers to questions 5 and 6. The faith of Thomas is the climax of the Gospel. John's message to readers (including us) is to stop doubting and believe.

7. Where have we seen this message before? This is an opportunity to review

what we have learned so far from the conversations of Jesus in John's Gospel. It may help to point people to the following verses: 3 v 14-18; 4 v 42; 6 v 29, 35, 40, 47; 9 v 39; 11 v 25-26; 18 v 37. Throughout John's Gospel there is a call to believe in Jesus and the truth to which He testifies. And throughout the Gospel there is the promise that those who believe in Jesus will receive eternal life.

8. We cannot touch Jesus as Thomas did. What evidence can we base our faith on? V 31: Our faith is built on the written testimony of the first apostles = the New Testament. You may want to look back at 2 v 18-25, and ask the following questions:

⌄

• **Upon what is the faith of the disciples based?** The disciples believe when they remember the words of Jesus and Scripture.
• **What does Jesus make of faith that arises from seeing miracles?** Jesus doesn't trust faith that arises from seeing miracles—probably because it may fade when things get tough.

EXPLORE MORE
Read 1 John 1 v 1-4. What parallels are there with the story of Thomas? 1 John emphasises that the apostles were able to see, hear and touch Jesus. Perhaps John has Thomas in mind when he talks of touching Jesus. Now the apostles testify to the truth about Jesus and proclaim it to others so they too might believe (paralleling John 20 v 29-31). Those who believe receive eternal life (paralleling John 20 v 31).

9. APPLY: How would Thomas respond to the quote in Q1? Thomas would strongly refute the idea that he believed just because he imagined it to be true. And he would strongly refute the idea that what he believed was just a metaphor. He was not credulous or gullible. He demanded proof.

10. APPLY: Is it true that "seeing is believing"? Look at v 29. Jesus says those who believe without seeing are blessed. Again this is an opportunity to review what we have seen previously in John's Gospel. See 9 v 39. Those who see are often blind to the truth. See 11 v 45-48. Some who saw Lazarus rise from the dead still chose to reject Jesus (see 12 v 37). See 3 v 19-20. We reject the light because we don't want to be exposed and we don't want to accept the implication that Jesus is Lord.

11. APPLY: What do verses 19, 21 and 26 all have in common? What is the implication for us? In each, Jesus says: "Peace be with you!" The One who is Lord and God is not against us, but for us. His rule as Lord means He can care for His people. "Stop doubting and believe" is a call for someone to begin to follow Jesus. But it is also a daily call for Christians. We need to believe day by day that Jesus forgives our sin without us needing to prove ourselves, and to believe that Jesus cares for us.

12. APPLY: What are the implications spelled out in verses 21-23? The resurrection creates a new purpose: we are sent. We are given the Holy Spirit. Just as God breathed His breath into dust at creation and gave life to Adam (Genesis 2 v 7), so Jesus breathes His breath into the disciples and gives new life. The result is that forgiveness and judgment are enacted in the lives of people. This is because when we proclaim the message of Jesus we either soften or harden people. If they accept our message, their sins are forgiven. If they reject our message, their sins are not forgiven.

13. What is the promise of verse 31? If the One who died for us is now alive, then we can have life in His name. The result of believing is life! We will share the resurrection life of Jesus. See also 3 v 16; 4 v 14; 5 v 24; 6 v 47; 11 v 25-26.

OPTIONAL EXTRA

To finish off the series, review the key points learned about Jesus from each session. Give people the opportunity to share which truth has impacted them most and talk about the differences in everyday life that come from knowing and believing these truths.